Also by Rosemary Ellen Guiley

Tales of Reincarnation
Angels of Mercy
The Miracle of Prayer

BLESSINGS

Prayers for the Home and Family

COMPILED BY

Rosemary Ellen Guiley

POCKET BOOKS

New York   London   Toronto   Sydney   Tokyo   Singapore

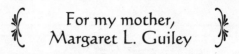

For my mother,
Margaret L. Guiley

An *Original* Publication of POCKET BOOKS

POCKET BOOKS, a division of Simon & Schuster Inc.
1230 Avenue of the Americas, New York, NY 10020

Blessings : prayers for the home and family / compiled by Rosemary
    Ellen Guiley.
        p.   cm.
    Includes bibliographical references.
    ISBN 0-671-53713-X
    1. Family—Prayer-books and devotions—English.   I. Guiley,
Rosemary.
    BL625.6.B54   1996
    291.4'3—dc20   96-41464
                                                                CIP

First Pocket Books hardcover printing December 1996

10 9 8 7 6 5 4 3 2 1

POCKET and colophon are registered trademarks of Simon & Schuster Inc.

Jacket design by Gina DiMarco
Text design by Stanley S. Drate/Folio Graphics Co. Inc.

Printed in the U.S.A.

Contents

Introduction

Prayer is love in action, and there is no greater force in the universe than love. The unconditional love of God flows in eternal currents throughout the universe, uniting everything that is. Prayer helps us to tap into those currents, so that we become channels, bringing unconditional love into manifestation.

When we pray, mighty forces move. Prayer helps us overcome life's obstacles. It helps give us peace of mind, and helps us find our own strength. Prayer helps us build our spiritual house. Ultimately, prayer helps us remember who we are. When we remember who we are, we become the love of God. Bayazid al-Bistāmī, a renowned Sufi mystic of the ninth century, observed, "A single atom of the love of God in a heart is worth more than a hundred thousand paradises."

This book is a collection of prayers for that which we hold nearest and dearest to us in life, the home, and family. There are prayers to begin and end the day, graces for meals, prayers for rites of passage and special occasions, for marital union and love, for childbirth and child rearing, for domestic happiness, for work, school, loved ones and friends, pets, and travel.

The prayers included herein were chosen for their ability to inspire and uplift and for their affirmation of the good in life and the human spirit and of the wholeness of the universe. To raise ourselves up, both individually and as a collective of the human soul, we must emphasize the positive, the good, the love. When we start the day with affirmative prayer, we are energized throughout the day. When we end the day with affirmative prayer, we fertilize our dreams, a source of healing and creativity.

Sources for this collection include faiths around the world throughout history. There are ancient prayers and modern prayers. We have called God by many names, we have worshiped God in many ways. We have prayed in many ways. All names, all worship, all prayer, lead back to the Source. Our desire to reunite with God is universal. The origins of the prayers are given, and, when known, the dates or time periods of their creation. Many of the prayers come out of oral traditions with no fixed dates. Prayers of recent origins are labeled "modern."

The labels are instructive for seeing the universality of our approaches to God, for realizing that we are fundamentally the same in our spiritual striving. The day will come when labels will no longer be necessary, and will fall away. We will simply look at all prayer as *prayer,* and we will allow it all to resonate within the heart without thought of boundaries between us and another.

—ROSEMARY ELLEN GUILEY

Annapolis, 1996

1

Home Blessings and Family Happiness

On Setting Up a New Home

O Lord God of our fathers, Giver of life and love, give thy blessing to us whom thou hast drawn together in love; surround us with thy protecting care; build thou for us our home; make it to be the abode of light and love. May all that is pure, tender, and true grow up under its shelter; may all that hinders godly union and concord, be driven far from it. Make it the center of fresh, sweet, and holy influence. Give us wisdom for life, and discretion in the guidance of our affairs. Let thy Fatherly hand ever be over us, and thy Holy Spirit ever be with us. O Lord, bless us and ours, and grant us all to inherit thine everlasting Kingdom.

(Christian, date unknown)

Prayer for Entering a New House

My father built,
And his father built,
And I have built.
Leave me to live here in success,
Let me sleep in comfort,
And have children.
There is food for you.

(Uganda, date unknown)

Dedication for a New Home

May the house wherein I dwell be blessed;
My good thoughts here possess me;
May my path of life be straight and true;
My dreams as here I lie be joyous;
All above, below, about me
May the house I love be hallowed.

(Omaha, date unknown)

Dedicating a New Homestead

B less this tree, make it grow, let it be entirely a blessing without any evil. Remove all evil, let it not come but let only the good come. Give thy blessing that we may increase in all things and grow wealthy and be free from disease. Let blessings abound.

(Banyoro, Uganda, date unknown)

Blessing a New House

May the person who is going to live in this house have many children; may he [she] be rich; may he be honest to people and good to the poor; may he not suffer from disease or any other kind of trouble; may he be safe all these years.

(Nyole [Abaluyia], Kenya, date unknown)

Consecration of a New House

May we stay well in this country; we did not know that we would arrive here. May we stay with peace and dream honey (i.e., have pleasant dreams); the God of old, the sun, when it rises in the east, may it bring us honey, and when it goes to set in the west may it take the badness with it.

(Nyole [Abaluyia], Kenya, date unknown)

Improvised Song of Joy

Ajaja-aja-jaja,
The lands around my dwelling
Are more beautiful
From the day
When it is given to me to see
Faces I have never seen before.
All is more beautiful,
All is more beautiful,
And life is thankfulness.
These guests of mine
Make my house grand,
Ajaja-aja-jaja.

(Iglulik Eskimo, date unknown)

When Covering the Fire

I preserve this fire as Christ preserveth me,
   May Mary at the top of the house, and Bride
   in its center be,
May the eight most powerful angels in the City of Grace
Protect this house and bring its people safe.

(Gaelic oral tradition, date unknown)

When Making a Bed

This bed I make
   In the name of the Father, and of the Son,
   and of the Holy Spirit;
In the name of the night we were conceived;
In the name of the day we were baptised;
In the name of every night, every day, every season,
And of every angel that is in Heaven.

(Gaelic oral tradition, date unknown)

Bless Our Family

Regard, O Lord, with Thy favor all the members of this household. Bind us together in love, sympathy and forbearance. Brighten our daily existence with those endearing graces that come from Thee. Help us to live each for the other, and to find our happiness in doing good and denying ourselves.

(Christian, date unknown)

Smiling in Good Fortune

Let me smile in good fortune;
Let my children smile in good fortune;
Let my home smile in good fortune.
I do not eat what is not mine.
I do not steal my neighbors' goods.
I always wish good health to others.
I am never in debt.
He who hates me is unjust.
I am always smiling in good fortune.

(Banyankore, Uganda, date unknown)

For Domestic Happiness

Let peace abound in our small company. Purge out of every heart the lurking grudge. Give us grace and strength to forbear and to persevere. Offenders ourselves, give us the grace to accept and to forgive offenders. Forgetful, help us to bear cheerfully the forgetfulness of others. Give us courage and gaiety and the quiet mind.

(Christian, date unknown)

Bless This Household

O eternal God, who alone makest men to be of one mind in a house; Help us, the members of this household, faithfully to fulfill our duties to thee and to each other. Put far from us all unkind thoughts, anger and evil speaking. Give us tender hearts, full of affection and sympathy toward all. Grant us grace to feel the sorrows and trials of others as our own, and to bear patiently with their imperfections. Preserve us from selfishness, and grant that, day by day, walking in love, we may grow up into the likeness of thy blessed Son, and be found ready to meet him, and to enter with him into that place which he has gone to prepare for us; for his sake, who liveth and reigneth with thee and the Holy Ghost ever, one God, world without end.

(Christian, date unknown)

Near and Dear

Be gracious to all that are near and dear to me, and keep us all in thy fear and love. Guide us, good Lord, and govern us by the same Spirit, that we may be so united to thee here as not to be divided when thou art pleased to call us hence, but may together enter into thy glory, through Jesus Christ, our blessed Lord and Saviour, who hath taught us when we pray to say: Our Father . . .

(John Wesley, Christian, 1703–1791)

For the Household

O Almighty God, look graciously upon this household as we are now gathered together in thy name. Give them whom thou has set over it, wisdom to direct those committed to their charge; give to all its members strength to fulfill thy will in the daily work to which thou has appointed them; grant that love and peace with all other graces may live and grow among them, and that finally we may meet before thy throne in heaven, and be united in thy love forever.

(Christian, date unknown)

Humble Home

O blessed Jesus, who for thirty years didst dwell in thy humble home at Nazareth, be with us in our homes. Keep from them all pride and selfishness and impurity, that they may be dwellings fit for thy sacred presence. Grant us to grow in grace and in the knowledge of thee.

(Christian, date unknown)

Prayer on Relatives

This afternoon, Lord, I must begin
my annual round of visiting relatives,
Checking them off as I go
so that I don't slight any.
Visiting friends is pleasant, Lord,
it's relaxing, it's renewing;
but visiting relatives
who are little more than strangers
is an obligation that you're born with
or marry into,
which usually ends up being nothing
but a drain on the nervous system.

They show you their cat
which hates you instantly,
or their nervous canary
which turns sullen and refuses to sing;
they take you down to the cellar
to inspect their damson preserves,

or upstairs to view the attic
they show you the fine points of sewing.
All I ask, Lord, is the grace
to sit through it without yawning,
because my slim once a year visit
may mean more to them
than I'll ever know.

(Max Pauli, Christian, modern)

For Family Success

Lord, behold our family here assembled. We thank thee for this place in which we dwell; for the love that unites us; for the peace accorded us this day; for the hope with which we expect the morrow; for the health, the work, the food and the bright skies, that make our lives delightful; for our friends in all parts of the earth, and our friendly helpers in this foreign isle. Let peace abound in our small company. Purge out of every heart the lurking grudge. Give us grace and strength to forbear and to persevere. Offenders ourselves, give us the grace to accept and to forgive offenders. Forgetful ourselves, help us to bear cheerfully the forgetfulness of others. Give us courage and gaiety and a quiet mind. Spare to us our friends, soften to us our enemies. Bless us, if it may be, in all our innocent endeavours. If it may not, give us the strength to encounter that which is to come, that we be brave in peril, constant in tribulation, temperate in wrath, and in all changes of fortune, and, down to the gates of death, loyal and loving one to another. As the clay to the potter, as the windmill to the wind, as children of their sire, we beseech of thee this help and mercy.

(Robert Louis Stevenson, 1850–1894)

For Peace

Peace between neighbors,
Peace between kindred,
Peace between lovers,
In the love of the King of life.

Peace between person and person,
Peace between wife and husband,
Peace between women and children,
The peace of Christ above all peace.

Bless, O Christ, my face,
Let my face bless everything;
Bless, O Christ, mine eye,
Let mine eye bless all it sees.

(Gaelic, date unknown)

A Child's Prayer for Family and Friends

Lord Jesus Christ,
I praise and thank you for my parents and
my brothers and sisters,
whom you have given me to cherish.
Surround them with your tender, loving care,
teach them to love and serve one another
in true affection,
and to look to you in all their needs.
I place them all in your care,
knowing that your love for them is greater
than my own.
Keep us close to one another in this life
and conduct us at the last to our true
and heavenly home.
Blessed be God for ever. Amen.

(Christian, date unknown)

May I Be a Blessing

In my home life may I be a blessing; its sunbeam when the days are dark; its inspiration when the days are sad and hopeless; its tender comfort when the days are full of pain and tears. Always thinking of others before myself; never imposing my private sorrows; ever with the girt loin and the lighted torch; washing my face and anointing my eyes, and confiding my griefs to Thee only, that I may ever have a heart at leisure from itself to soothe and sympathize.

(Abbie C. Morrow, 1902, adapted)

Prayer for Family

God of I AM, with the thought that I must lift myself up, I pray for all the encompassing outwardly reaching Joy contained in Love. Not your Love for me My God in which I implicitly trust, but your Love in me overflowing and manifesting from me. May I be a co-creator with you my God. May I touch and hold and cherish what I was once too ignorant to see. And let me remember my God, that of all the people to whom kindness should be shown I pray that I share the best with my loved ones. I pray that when lessons to learn burn the soul—that cooling patience, unshakable Love and ultimate trust play their parts. I pray for faith that the kingdom of heaven manifest in my being and that my actions being guided by my ideals be really You in disguise. I pray for the wisdom to know the path, to feel the path, to share the path with my wife, my family and my friends. So Be It Now My God, Your Love within me free.

(Thomas Wright, modern)

A Birthday Prayer

May my heart hold the love of little children, of old age and of frail and wavering ones, fragile in faith and purpose. May my arms be strong to give assistance and shelter, and may my understanding grow day by day until the world is blessed by my work. Help me to foster those ideals and dreams which will materialize into beautiful realities, and may I picture those things of the spirit which will bring this to pass. Rapidly or slowly as my progress may come, let me ever be ready to give of what I have in such great abundance.

(Elinor Cochrane Stewart, modern)

On a Birthday

Every passing year makes my life shorter and time that is gone can never be recalled. Assist me, Ahura Mazda, to be wise from the experiences of the past and to move into the future with joy and hope. Guide me to make the best use of each day and each opportunity as they come so that I may glorify the name of my ancestors, my religion, my community and my country. Grant me Thy clear and pure mind, I pray, and devotion to Thee in everything I say or do. May the heavenly sun light my way for many a year to come and may Thy love and blessings always be with me in life. May I always remain worthy of Thy love!

(Zoroastrian, c. sixth century B.C.)

2

Table Blessings

Before a Meal

Most gracious God, who hast given us Christ and with him all that is necessary to life and godliness: we thankfully take this our food as the gift of thy bounty, procured by his merits. Bless it to the nourishment and strength of our frail bodies to fit us for thy cheerful service.

(Richard Baxter, Christian, 1615–1691)

Before Food

May the blessing of the five loaves and two fishes which God divided amongst the five thousand men, be ours; and may the King Who made the division put luck on our food and on our portion.

(Christian, date unknown)

Recitation Before Meals

In the name of God, the Compassionate, the Merciful.
Glory be to Thee Who dividest Thy provisions
and Who forgetest us not in Thy favors.

(Druze, date unknown)

Table Blessing

May the Merciful One bless the host and hostess and all who are seated about the table . . . just as our forefathers were blessed in every way with every manner of blessing.

(Jewish, date unknown)

Before a Meal

O Lord, who is the giver of all good things, fill our hearts with gratitude for the food and drink laid before us. And as we fill our bellies, may we be sober and frugal in our eating, taking only that which is necessary to refresh ourselves for your service. Let the pleasure we take in the bread which nourishes our earthly bodies, be as nothing to the joy we take in the spiritual bread of your truth, which nourishes the soul.

(John Calvin, Christian, 1509–1564)

Grace for a Child

What God gives, and what we take,
'Tis a gift for Christ His sake:
Be the meale of Beanes and Pease,
God be thank'd for those, and these:
Have we flesh, or have we fish,
All are Fragments from His dish.
He His Church save, and the King,
And our Peace here, like a Spring,
Make it ever flourishing.

(English verse, date unknown)

At the Table

Lord Christ, we ask you to spread our table with your mercy. And may you bless with your gentle hands the good things you have given us. We know that whatever we have comes from your lavish heart, for all that is good comes from you. Thus whenever we eat, we should give thanks to you. And having received from your hands, let us give with equally generous hands to those who are poor, breaking bread and sharing our bread with them. For you have told us that whatever we give to the poor, we give to you.

(Alcuin of York, Christian, c. 735–804)

Before Eating

May rivers continue to flow, may clouds rain, may plants produce good fruit, may I be the lord of lands that produce food, rice, and curds.

(Hindu, Taittīriya Brāhmana *II.7.16.4)*

Morning Meal

Infinite Father, at this morning meal draw us near to Thee. Help us to open our minds and hearts that we may receive Thy spirit and be guided through the changing scenes of this new day in perfect security, and, when the night shadows fall, may we find ourselves in harmony with Thee. And, day by day, may we so live that we will grow continually into the likeness of our Maker.

(Christian, date unknown)

Morning Meal

D ear Father, we thank Thee for Thy care over us through the night; let us live this day as if it were to be our last. Bless this breakfast and bless our lives.

(Christian, date unknown)

Noon Meal

Glorious God, Thou Great Sun of righteousness, we gratefully remember Thee at this mid-day meal. As the sun at its meridian height is the beauty and glory of the day, so may Thy glory and mercy shine down upon us to warm our hearts and quicken our consciences to do Thy will, that at the close of this day we may ask Thy blessing upon all our acts and lie down to peaceful slumber in the full consciousness of duty well done.

(Christian, date unknown)

Noon Meal

Mighty Father, in gratefulness at this noon day meal, we also thank Thee that, each day, we have something to do, and that, by doing these things, to the best of our ability, we may acquire the virtues of temperance, self control, diligence, cheerfulness, contentment and all the other graces that become Thy followers. May we be ever diligent about our Father's business.

(Christian, date unknown)

Evening Meal

Great Father, we are devoutly thankful this evening for material blessings, but we also humbly ask to be fed with the bread of Heaven that we may be strong of mind, pure of heart, fearless of action and ever ready to follow wheresoever Thou shalt lead.

(Christian, date unknown)

Evening Meal

Dear Shepherd of our souls, we thank Thee at this closing meal of the day, for these evidences of Thy care and for having so mercifully protected us. We entreat Thee to forgive our sins. We pray Thy fatherly care over us during the coming night. Into Thy keeping we commend our souls, our bodies, our all, knowing that the "Eternal God is our refuge and underneath are the everlasting arms." In the good Shepherd's Name.

(Christian, date unknown)

Grace After a Small Repast

Blessed art Thou, O Lord,
our God, King of the World,
Creator of many living beings
and their wants.
We thank Thee for all what Thou hast created
to restore therewith the life of all living beings.
Blessed be He, who lives in eternity.

(Jewish, date unknown)

When Guests Are Present

Almighty God, we thank Thee for the food we are about to receive. Bless our guest(s) with us at this table. Enrich our lives by these happy associations. Pour Thy Holy Spirit into our hearts, and may we lead lives of trust, faith, obedience and love. Bless us all and all families represented here.

(Christian, date unknown)

When Someone Is Absent from the Table

All wise and all seeing God Who are present everywhere, we extend to Thee our thanks for food and all Thy mercies. We ask Thy blessing and care over the one absent from this table, our dear (father, mother, brother, sister or friend, giving name). Guide, direct and keep him in Thy ways at all times and in all places; and, if it be according to Thy will, return him to us in safety through Thy goodness.

(Christian, date unknown)

A Birthday Table Blessing

Almighty God, we thank Thee for our daily bread and for the life of (name) the one whose birthday anniversary we celebrate today. Grant him health, grace, happiness and Thy guidance through a long, worthy and useful life and, at its earthly end, may he come into Thy kingdom of everlasting life and glory.

(Christian, date unknown)

After a Meal

We give thanks, O God and Father, for the many mercies which you constantly bestow upon us. In supplying the food and drink necessary to sustain our present life, you show how much you care for our mortal bodies. And in supplying the life and the teachings of your Son, you reveal how much you love our immortal souls. Let the meal which we have enjoyed be a reminder to us of the eternal joy you promise to all who feed on your holy Word.

(John Calvin, Christian, 1509–1564)

After Food

Praise to the generous King,
  Unceasing praise to God,
And praise to Jesus Christ
For what we have had of food.

(Christian, date unknown)

Blessing for Table

Be known to us in breaking bread,
   But do not *then* depart.
Savior abide with us and spread
   Thy table in each heart.

(German grace, date unknown)

After a Meal

Most merciful Father, accept of our thanks for these and all thy mercies; and give us yet more thankful hearts. O give us more of the great mercies proper to thy children, even thy sanctifying and comforting Spirit and assurance of thy love through Christ.

(Richard Baxter, Christian, 1615–1691)

3

Prayers to Begin the Day

We Rise Up in the Morning

W e rise up in the morning before the day, to betake ourselves to our labor, to prepare our harvest. Protect us from the dangerous animal and from the serpent, and from every stumbling block.

(Nandi, Kenya, date unknown)

To Meet the Tasks of the Day

Father, I thank thee for thy mercies which are new every morning. For the gift of sleep; for health and strength; for the vision of another day with its fresh opportunities of work and service; for all these and more than these, I thank thee. Before looking on the face of men I would look on thee, who art the health of my countenance and my God. Not without thy guidance would I go forth to meet the duties and tasks of the day. Strengthen me so that in all my work I may be faithful; amid trials, courageous; in suffering, patient; under disappointment, full of hope in thee. Grant this for thy goodness' sake.

(Samuel McComb, date unknown)

Lord, Remember Me

O Lord, thou knowest how busy we must be this day; if we forget thee, do not thou forget us; for Christ's sake.

(General Lord Astley, 1579–1652)

Thanksgiving for a New Day

We give thee hearty thanks, O God, for the rest of the past night and for the gift of a new day with its opportunities of pleasing thee. Grant that we so pass its hours in the perfect freedom of thy service, that at eventide we may again give thanks unto thee; through Jesus Christ our Lord.

(Daybreak Office of the Eastern Church, third century)

A Child's Morning Prayer

Father we thank Thee for the night,
And for the pleasant morning light;
For rest and food and loving care,
All that makes the day so fair.

Help us to do the things we should,
To be to others kind and good,
In all we do, in work or play,
To grow more loving every day.

(Abbie C. Morrow, 1902)

For a Happy Day

Po! God, may the day dawn well;
May you spit upon us the medicine
So that we may walk well!

(Vugusu, Kenya, date unknown)

Prayer for the Day

O God, as the day returns and brings us the petty round of irritating duties, help us to perform them with laughter and kind faces; let cheerfulness abound with industry. Give us to go blithely on our business all this day, bring us to our resting beds weary and content and undishonored, and grant us in the end the gift of sleep.

(Robert Louis Stevenson, 1850–1894)

The Salutation of the Dawn

Listen to the exhortation of
   the Dawn!
Look to this Day! For it is Life,
   The very Life of Life.
In its brief course lie all Varieties
And Realities of your Existence;
   The Bliss of Growth,
   The Glory of Action,
   The Splendor of Beauty;
For Yesterday is but a Dream,
And Tomorrow is only a Vision;
   But To-day well-lived
Makes every Yesterday a Dream of
   Happiness,
And ever To-morrow a Vision of
   Hope.
Look well therefore to this Day!
Such is the Salutation of the Dawn.

(Hindu, date unknown)

In the Morning

O God, I enter in the morning in need of Thee,
powerless and unable to avoid what I dislike,
and incapable of accomplishing what I want, except with Thy help.
O God, I enter the morning pledged for what I have done.
Everything is in Thy hand.
I am most in need of Thee,
and Thou are most independent of any being.
Make not, O God, my enemies to gloat over me.
Protect my friends from any misfortune
and me from the misfortunes of unbelief.
Let me not be concerned with worldly endeavor.
I pray that on Judgment Day I will have been
     worthy of Thy sanction through Thy mercy.
O God, Thou art the most merciful of the merciful.

(Druze, date unknown)

At Daybreak

Lord Jesus Christ, you are the sun that always rises, but never sets. You are the source of all life, creating and sustaining every living thing. You are the source of all food, material and spiritual, nourishing us in both body and soul. You are the light that dispels the clouds of error and doubt, and goes before me every hour of the day, guiding my thoughts and my actions. May I walk in your light, be nourished by your food, be sustained by your mercy, and be warmed by your love.

(Erasmus, Christian, 1466–1536)

For a Day Full of Blessings

O, sun,
As you rise in the east through God's leadership,
Wash away all the evil of which I have thought throughout the night.
Bless me, so that my enemies will not kill me and my family;
Guide me through hard work.
O God, give me mercy upon our children who are suffering:
Bring riches today as the sun rises;
Bring all fortunes to me today.

(Abaluyia, Kenya, date unknown)

On Rising

Rule over me this day, O God, leading me on the path of righteousness. Put your Word in my mind and your Truth in my heart, that this day I neither think nor feel anything except what is good and honest. Protect me from all lies and falsehood, helping me to discern deception wherever I meet it. Let my eyes always look straight ahead on the road you wish me to tread, that I might not be tempted by any distraction. And make my eyes pure, that no false desires may be awakened within me.

(Jacob Boehme, Christian, 1575–1624)

For Morning

O God, the Father of lights, from whom cometh down every good and perfect gift: We thank thee for thy gracious care this past night, and pray that this day we may serve thee with all our strength and might.

(Christian, date unknown)

Into Your Hands

I nto your hands, O Lord, we commend ourselves this day. Let your presence be with us to its close. Strengthen us to remember that in whatsoever good work we do we are serving you. Give us a diligent and watchful spirit, that we may seek in all things to know your will, and knowing it, gladly to perform it, to the honor and glory of your name; through Jesus Christ our Lord.

(Gelasian Sacramentary, Christian, c. 500)

Morning Prayer

I reverently speak in the presence of the Great Parent God: I pray that this day, the whole day, as a child of God, I may not be taken hold of by my own desire, but show forth the divine glory by living a life of creativeness, which shows forth the true individual.

(Shinto, date unknown)

Let Me Pass the Day in Peace

O God, thou hast let me pass the night in peace,
Let me pass the day in peace.
Wherever I may go
Upon my way which thou madest peaceable for me,
O God, lead my steps.
When I have spoken,
Keep off calumny from me.
When I am hungry,
Keep me from murmuring.
When I am satisfied,
Keep me from pride.
Calling upon thee, I pass the day,
O Lord who hast no Lord.

(Kenya, date unknown)

The Greatest of All Lights

O God, creator of light: at the rising of your sun this morning, let the greatest of all lights, your love, rise like the sun within our hearts.

(Armenian Apostolic Church, Christian, date unknown)

Self-baptism for the Morning
(Recited while sprinkling water on the head.)

O Waters, give us health, bestow on us
Vigor and strength, so shall I see enjoyment.
Rain down your dewy treasures o'er our path.
Like loving mothers, pour on us your blessing,
Make us partakers of your sacred essence.
We come to you for cleansing from all guilt,
Cause us to be productive, make us prosper.

(Hindu, Rig-Veda *X.9)*

Kindling Prayer

I will kindle my fire this morning
In the presence of the holy angels of heaven,
In the presence of Ariel of the loveliest form,
In the presence of Uriel of the myriad charms,
Without malice, without jealousy, without envy,
Without fear, without terror of anyone under the sun,
But the Holy Son of God to shield me.
   Without malice, without jealousy, without envy,
   Without fear, without terror of any one under the sun,
   But the Holy Son of God to shield me.

God, kindle Thou in my heart within
A flame of love to my neighbor,
To my foe, to my friend, to my kindred all,
To the brave, to the knave, to the thrall,
O Son of the loveliest Mary,
From the lowliest thing that liveth,
To the Name that is highest of all.

(Gaelic oral tradition, Christian, date unknown)

4

Prayers to End the Day

At Day's End

O Lord our God, Who alone makest us to dwell in safety; refresh with quiet sleep this night those who are wearied with the labors of the day; and mercifully protect from harm all who put their trust in Thee; that lying down in peace to take our rest, we may fear no evil, but confidently give ourselves into Thy holy keeping.

(Christian, date unknown)

At Night

Lord Jesus Christ, you are the gentle moon and joyful stars, that watch over the darkest night. You are the source of all peace, reconciling the whole universe to the Father. You are the source of all rest, calming troubled hearts, and bringing sleep to weary bodies. You are the sweetness that fills our minds with quiet joy, and can turn the worst nightmares into dreams of heaven. May I dream of your sweetness, rest in your arms, be at one with your Father, and be comforted in the knowledge that you always watch over me.

(Erasmus, Christian, 1466–1536)

O God Incline Thy Ear

O God do thou thine ear incline,
Protect my children and my kine,
Even if thou art weary, still forbear
And hearken to my constant prayer.
When shrouded beneath the cloak of night,
Thy splendors sleep beyond our sight,
And when the sky by day,
Thou movest, still to thee I pray,
Dread shades of our departed sires,
Ye who can make or mar desires,
Slain by no mortal hand ye dwell,
Beneath the earth, O guard us well.

(Nandi, Kenya, date unknown)

Holy Angels Guard Our Sleep

O Christ, Son of the living God,
May your holy angels guard our sleep.
May they watch us as we rest
And hover around our beds.

Let them reveal to us in our dreams
Visions of your glorious truth,
O High Prince of the universe,
O High Priest of the mysteries.

May no dreams disturb our rest
And no nightmares darken our dreams.
May no fears or worries delay
Our willing, prompt repose.

May the virtue of our daily work
Hallow our nightly prayers.
May our sleep be deep and soft,
So our work be fresh and hard.

(Celtic oral tradition, date unknown)

Forgive Our Heedless Acts

Forgive me, most gracious Lord and Father, if this day I have done or said anything to increase the pain of the world. Pardon the unkind word, the impatient gesture, the hard and selfish deed, the failure to show sympathy and kindly help where I have had the opportunity but missed it; and enable me so to live that I may daily do something to lessen the tide of human sorrow, and add to the sum of human happiness.

(Christian, date unknown)

For a Quiet Night

The Lord Almighty grant us a quiet night and a perfect end.

(Christian, date unknown)

For Restoration

O Merciful Father, to Whose house of many mansions Thy child shall one day approach alone, by lying down to sleep; let Thy gentle renewing hands be upon me, and Thy loving eyes behold me, as I go to sleep this night. Thou Who givest Thy beloved sleep, grant that I may rest at peace with Thee, and with all Thy creatures. Renew my body, and cleanse my heart and soul, by Thy creative power, and grant that the morning light may make me rejoice alike in rendering new service to Thee, and in being one day nearer to the vision of Thy face.

(Christian, date unknown)

Refreshed in Body, Mind and Soul

O Lord God, who has given us the night for rest, I pray that in my sleep my soul may remain awake to you, steadfastly adhering to your love. As I lay aside my cares to relax and relieve my mind, may I not forget your infinite and unresting care for me. And in this way, let my conscience be at peace, so that when I rise tomorrow, I am refreshed in body, mind and soul.

(John Calvin, Christian, 1509–1564)

Evening Blessing

Blessed art Thou, Lord our God, King of the universe, who with His
   word brings on the evenings,
With wisdom Opens the gates,
With understanding alters the phases, varies the seasons,
And arranges the stars in their heavenly orbit according to His will.
He creates days and night.
He rolls away the light from before the darkness and the darkness
   from before the light,
He makes the day to pass and the night to come, and divides between
   day and night;
Lord of hosts is His name.
A living and everlasting God, who shall constantly reign over us
   forever and ever.
Blessed art Thou Lord, who brings on the evenings.

(Jewish, date unknown)

Evening Prayer

I reverently speak in the presence of the Great Parent God: I give you grateful thanks that you have enabled me to live this day, the whole day, in obedience to the excellent spirit of your ways.

(Shinto, date unknown)

At Evening

I thank you, O God, for your care and protection this day, keeping me from physical harm and spiritual corruption. I now place the work of the day into your hands, trusting that you will redeem my errors and turn my achievements to your glory. And I now ask you to work within me, trusting that you will use the hours of rest to create in me a new heart and new soul. Let my mind, which through the day has been directed to my work, through the evening be wholly directed at you.

(Jacob Boehme, Christian, 1575–1624)

In the Evening

Now that the sun has set,
I sit and rest, and think of you.
Give my weary body peace.
Let my legs and arms stop aching.
Let my nose stop sneezing,
Let my head stop thinking.
Let me sleep in your arms.

(Dinka, date unknown)

The Quiet Hours of the Night

O God, who gives the day for work and the night for sleep, refresh our bodies and our minds through the quiet hours of night, and let our inward eyes be directed towards you, dreaming of your eternal glory.

(Leonine Sacramentary, Christian, fifth century)

Evening Prayer

O Almighty Father, who givest the sun for a light by day and the ordinances of the moon and the stars for a light by night: Vouchsafe to receive us this night and ever into thy favor and protection, ruling and governing us by thy Holy Spirit, that all darkness and error may be removed far from us, and that we may stand fast in thy commandments and ever hold thy judgments in firm remembrance. Give us grace this night and ever to celebrate thy praise, to bless thee, and to magnify thy Name; and to thee be glory for ever and ever.

(Christian, date unknown)

Let Me Pass the Night in Peace

O God, thou hast let me pass the day in peace,
Let me pass the night in peace,
O Lord who hast no Lord.
There is no strength but in thee.
Thou alone has no obligation.
Under thy hand I pass the night.
Thou art my mother and my father.

(Kenya, date unknown)

Bed Blessing

The Sacred Three
To save
To shield
To surround
The hearth
The house
The household
This eve
This night
O! this eve
This night
And every night
Each single night.
 Amen.

(Gaelic oral tradition, date unknown)

Before Sleep

I lie in my bed
As I would lie in the grave,
Thine arm beneath my neck,
Thou Son of Mary victorious.

Angels shall watch me
And I lying in slumber,
And angels shall guard me
In the sleep of the grave.

Uriel shall be at my feet,
Ariel shall be at my back,
Gabriel shall be at my head,
And Raphael shall be at my side.

Michael shall be with my soul,
The strong shield of my love!
And the Physician Son of Mary

Shall put the salve to mine eye,
The Physician Son of Mary
Shall put the salve to mine eye!

(Gaelic oral tradition, date unknown)

5

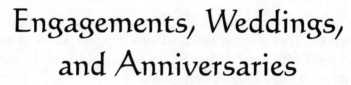

Engagements, Weddings, and Anniversaries

For a Fiancée

That I may come near to her, draw me nearer to thee than to her; that I may know her, make me to know thee more than her; that I may love her with the perfect love of a perfectly whole heart, cause me to love thee more than her and most of all. Amen. Amen.

That nothing may come between me and her, be thou between us, every moment. That we may be constantly together, draw us into separate loneliness with thyself. And when we meet breast to breast, my God, let it be on thine own. Amen. Amen.

(Temple Gairdner of Cairo, 1873–1928)

Epithalamium on a Late Happy Marriage

When *Hymen* once the mutual Bands has wove,
Exchanging Heart for Heart, and Love for Love,
The happy Pair, with mutual Bliss elate,
Own to be single's an imperfect State.
But when two Hearts united thus agree
With equal sense, and equal Constancy,
This, HAPPINESS, is thy extreamest Goal,
'Tis Marriage both of Body, and of Soul,
'Tis making Heav'n below with matchless Love,
And's a fair Step to reach the Heav'n above.

(Christopher Smart, 1722–1771)

Love Song

I know not whether thou hast been absent:
I lie down with thee, I rise up with thee,
In my dreams thou art with me.
If my eardrops tremble in my ears,
I know it is thou moving within my heart.

(Aztec, date unknown)

Thanksgiving for a Betrothal

We thank Thee, O Lord God Almighty, who art before the ages, Master of the universe, who didst adorn the heavens by thy word, and didst lay the foundation of the earth and all that is therein. Who didst gather together those things which were separate in union, and didst make the twain one. Now again, our Master, we beseech thee, may thy servants be worthy of the mark of the sign of thy Word through the bond of betrothal, their love one for another inviolable through the firm sureness of their union. Build them, O Lord, upon the foundation of thy Holy Church, that they may walk in conformity and accordance with the bond of the word which they have vowed to one another. For thou art the bond of their love, and the ordainer of the law of their union. Thou who hast brought about the oneness, by the union of the twain by thy words; complete, O Lord, the ordinance of thine only-begotton Son Jesus Christ our Lord.

(Coptic Christian, date unknown)

Night Singers

May the bridesmaids
all night long
sing of the love
of you and your bride,
adorned with violets.

(Sappho, c. 612 B.C.)

The Good-Night or Blessing

Blessings in abundance come
To the bride and to her groom;
May the bed and this short night
Know the fulness of delight!
Pleasures many here attend ye,
And, ere long, a boy Love send ye
Curled and comely, and so trim,
Maids in time may ravish him.
Thus a dew of graces fall
On ye both: good-night to all!

(Robert Herrick, 1591–1674)

Blessing for a Marriage

May your marriage bring you all the exquisite excitements
   a marriage should bring,
      and may life grant you also patience, tolerance, and
         understanding.
May you always need one another—
not so much to fill your emptiness as to help you to know your
      fullness.
A mountain needs a valley to be complete;
   the valley does not make the mountain less but more;
and the valley is more a valley because it has a mountain
      towering over it.
So let it be with you and you.
May you need one another, but not out of weakness.
May you want one another, but not out of lack.
May you entice one another, but not compel one another.
May you succeed in all important ways with one another,
   and not fail in the little graces.
May you look for things to praise, often say, "I love you!"
   and take no notice of small faults.

If you have quarrels that push you apart,
May both of you hope to have good sense enough to take the
first step back.
May you enter into the mystery which is the awareness of
one another's presence—
no more physical than spiritual, warm and near when you are
side by side,
and warm and near when you are in separate rooms or even
distant cities.
May you have happiness, and may you find it making one
another happy.
May you have love, and may you find it loving one another!
Thank you, God,
for Your presence here with us
and Your blessing on this marriage.
Amen.

(James Dillet Freeman, modern)

For a Marriage

Most merciful and gracious God, of whom the whole family in heaven and earth is named; bestow upon these thy servants the seal of thine approval, and thy fatherly benediction; granting them grace to fulfill, with pure and steadfast affection, the vow and covenant between them made. Guide them together, we beseech thee, in the happy way of righteousness and peace, that loving and serving thee, with one heart and mind, all the days of their life, they may be abundantly enriched with the tokens of thine everlasting grace, in Jesus Christ our Lord.

(Christian, date unknown)

A Wedding in the Home

O God, bless thy servants who are about to be joined together this day in holy matrimony; keep them, we beseech thee, under the protection of thy good providence, and make them to have a perpetual fear and love of thy holy name. Look, O Lord, mercifully upon them from heaven, and bless them; that they obeying thy will and alway [sic] being in safety under thy protection, may abide in thy love unto their lives' end.

(Christian, Ireland, 1895)

A Husband's Wedding Prayer
for Blessings and Happiness

Her soul, her eyes
Her caring self
God you gave to me
Like no one else

To your friend, O Lord
You know as me
Thank you God
For hearing my plea.

Now I shall walk
The garden path
Where flowers grow
Beside the grass

And learn the gentleness
That makes them grow

And with her God
Purify our souls.

Let two hearts my God
Sometimes seem as one
With colors and sparkles
Derived from the sun.

I love you God
And I will strive to be
A caring husband
With a knee to thee.

Bless us O Lord
And she who will be my wife
My lover, friend, companion
For the rest of this life.

(Thomas Wright, modern)

A Wedding

O God of profound mercy, in your great love,
you have willed that these two be joined together.
With your grace, two are made as one,
vowing to stay together to the end.

With hearts joined in unity,
together they will meet all trials and hardships,
together they will walk in the path of goodness
through the years
until white crowns their heads.

Faithfully they will follow your will
and purify their lives with Johrei.
Whatever obstacles loom ahead, these two
will overcome them in their love for each other,
and they will praise you more with each passing day.

From this day onward, O God,
help these two as they pledge their strength together
to build on this earth your paradise,
and bring them true happiness in their sacred travail.

(Johrei Fellowship, Japan, modern)

For a Wedding in the Home

O Lord God of our fathers, Giver of life and love, give Thy blessing to those whom Thou hast drawn together in love; surround them with Thy protecting care; build Thou for them their home; make it the abode of light and love. May all that is pure, tender and true, grow up under its shelter; may all that hinders godly union and concord, be driven far from it. Make it the center of fresh, sweet and holy influence. Give them wisdom for life, and discretion in the guidance of their affairs. Let Thy Fatherly hand ever be over them, and Thy Holy Spirit ever be with them. O Lord, bless them and theirs, and grant them to inherit Thine everlasting Kingdom.

(Bishop William Boyd Carpenter, b. 1841)

For Wife or Husband

Bless thy servant (my wife or husband) with health of body and of spirit. Let the hand of thy blessing be upon his head, night and day, and support him in all necessities, strengthen him in all temptations, comfort him in all his sorrows, and let him be thy servant in all changes; and make us both to dwell with thee for ever in thy favor, in the light of thy countenance, and in thy glory.

(Jeremy Taylor, Christian, 1613–1667)

To My Dear and Loving Husband

If ever two were one, then surely we.
If ever man were loved by wife, then thee;
If ever wife was happy in a man,
Compare with me, ye women, if you can.

I prize thy love more than whole mines of gold
Or all the riches that the East doth hold.
My love is such that rivers cannot quench,
Nor aught but love from thee, give recompense.

Thy love is such I can no way repay,
The heavens reward thee manifold, I pray.
Then while we live, in love let's so persevere
That when we live no more, we may live ever.

(Anne Bradstreet, ?1612–1672)

Marriage

We thank thee, O Lord God Almighty, who art before the ages, Master of the universe, who didst adorn the heavens by thy word, and didst lay the foundations of the earth and all that is therein. Who didst gather together those things which were separate into union, and didst make the twain one. Now again, our Master, we beseech thee, may thy servants be worthy of the mark of the sign of thy Word through the bond of betrothal, their love for one another inviolable through the firm sureness of their union. Build them, O Lord, upon the foundation of thy Holy Church, that they may walk in conformity and accordance with the bond of the word which they have vowed one to another. For thou art the bond of their love, and the ordainer of the law of their union. Thou who hast brought about the oneness, by the union of the twain by thy words; complete, O Lord, the ordinance of thine only-begotten Son Jesus Christ our Lord.

(Coptic Christian, date unknown)

For the Silver Wedding
(Twenty-five years)

Our hearts have been open unto Thee, Our God,
and Thou hast led us unto this happy hour.
   We have "never dreamed though right were worsted,
wrong would triumph."
   May the coming years be crowned with the glory
of Thy grace.
   For Thy loving care, and these abundant mercies,
we give Thee grateful praise.

(Edwin Hamlin Carr, modern)

For a Wedding Anniversary

O God, I thank you that you have given us another year of life together.

I thank you
   For the love which grows more precious and
   for the bonds which grow more close each day.

I thank you
   For the happiness we have known together;
   For the sorrows we have faced together;
   For all the experiences of sunshine and of shadow through which
    we have come today.

I ask your forgiveness
   For any disloyalty on my part;
   For any times when I was difficult to live with;
   For any selfishness and inconsiderateness;
   For any lack of sympathy and understanding;
   For anything which spoiled even for a moment
   the perfect relationship which marriage should be.

Spare us to each other to go on walking the way of life together,
   and grant that for us it may be true
   that the best is yet to be: through Jesus Christ my Lord.

(William Barclay, Christian, 1907–1978)

A Wedding Anniversary

O Lord, we are grateful for a day of celebration.
Another year has gone by with its experiences—
   good, bad, and indifferent.
We are together and thankful for our togetherness.
Through our life with each other
   we have so much for which to be thankful.
We have known all the intricate intimacies
   of two people learning to live together.
We have shared secrets together and have realized
   There are private places in each of us
   the other can never know.
We have known the ecstasy of physical union
   and the relief of temporary apartness.
We have quarreled and quickly made up.
We have quarreled and not made up
   until we realized
   that life without the other was empty.
We have laughed with each other
   and at each other.

We have prayed together.
We have learned how words can cut and wound
   and how words can soothe and comfort.
We have learned too
   that there are times when it is better to be silent.
We have felt upon occasion that our love was eternal,
   and wondered at times
If our marriage would last another week.
We have run the whole gamut of human emotions and feelings.
So, gratefully, O God, we celebrate it all—
   the loving and the sharing,
   the anger and the frustration,
   the giving and the taking,
   the fire and the ashes.
Bless by your Presence the renewal of our promise
and our covenant,
   in joy and in sorrow,
   in plenty and in want,
   in sickness and in health,
as long as we both shall live.

(Kenneth G. Phifer, modern)

The Golden Wedding
(Fifty years)

"Strong Son of God, immortal love;
  Whom we, that have not seen Thy face,
  By Faith, and faith alone, embrace,
Believing where we cannot prove."

It is Thou who hast showered blessings upon us
in the years gone by.
  The faith in our hearts is stronger for Thee
than ever; and as pure, we trust, as gold.
  Accept the gratitude of our souls for these, and
all the abundant mercies of life, granted to us
from Thy guiding hand. In Jesus' Name we humbly pray.

(Edwin Hamlin Carr, modern)

6

Childbirth and Rites
of Passage

Wishes for a Bridal Couple and Their Unborn Child

Soon may a noble offspring
Be born of you to Latium
To govern camp and courts
And create merry songs.

Cynthia, be thou kind,
Bless the tenth month with early fruit.
But, birth goddess, be thou merciful,
Let the pledge not wound the parent.

Unborn child, spare your mother's tender frame,
And when Nature has in secret carved your brow,
May you be born with features like your father's
But like your mother more.

And you, dear bride, the fairest of the realm,
Cherish the bond your worthy lord

Has sought so long to knit.
May your beauty never lessen,
May your youthful ardor linger,
And your loveliness be slow to fade.

(Ancient Roman verse)

A Midwife's Prayer

I take you out of the world of the spirits. Do not be sick, settle down, and may you have work.

(Giur, Sudan?, date unknown)

For a Baby

O Lord my God, shed the light of your love on my child. Keep him safe from all illness and all injury. Enter his tiny soul, and comfort him with your peace and joy. He is too young to speak to me, and to my ears his cries and gurgles are meaningless nonsense. But to your ears they are prayers. His cries are cries for your blessing. His gurgles are gurgles of delight at your grace. Let him as a child learn the way of your commandments. As an adult let him live the full span of life, serving your kingdom on earth. And finally in his old age let him die in the sure and certain knowledge of your salvation. I do not ask that he be wealthy, powerful or famous. Rather I ask that he be poor in spirit, humble in action, and devout in worship. Dear Lord, smile upon him.

(Johann Starck, Christian, 1680–1756)

For a New Child

Our Father, we ask thee to bless us. We thank thee for the new life that has come into our home. We bring it to thee in consecration. We would lay it in thine arms. We would ask for thy divine keeping of it. We cannot keep it, for the world is very full of evil. Thou alone canst guard it from harm. We ask thee for grace to make our home a fit place for this precious life to grow up in. Help us to make it a place of love, a place of prayer, a place of all beautiful living, a place sweet with heaven's fragrance. Make us fit to hold this child in our arms, to clasp it to our bosom, to be its teachers and guides. Help us to answer its questions, to solve its problems, and be to it a pattern of holy living.

(Christian, date unknown)

A Child's Investiture of the Sacred Tunic and Girdle

With the investiture of this tunic and girdle, we consign this child, dear Ahura Mazda, to thy love and care. Open his eyes, dear Lord, to his daily duties and help him in their loyal performance. Fill his mind with Thy thoughts and ideals, help him to live up to them and lead him from day unto day to be near their realization, O Divine Guide of all. Bless this child on this auspicious day of his life, dear Ahura Mazda, with Thy guidance, help and love, and give him a healthy body, a pure mind and a wide and noble outlook on life. Bless his parents, relatives and friends also with Thy kindness and love so that they can contribute substantially in molding this child and making him a good Zoroastrian and a good citizen of the world. Let this child, his parents and all those who are with and around him in life live in goodwill, understanding and mutual love throughout their tenure on earth.

(Zoroastrian, c. sixth century B.C.)

Prayer to the Earth Goddess at the Birth of a Child

Fellow men, we shall all live,
Earth Goddess, hear.
Whoever plants, let him dig up and eat.
Earth Goddess, hear.
We shall give birth to sons.
Earth Goddess, hear.
We shall give birth to daughters.
Earth Goddess, hear.
We shall train them.
Earth Goddess, hear.
When we are old they will feed us.
Earth Goddess, hear.
Whoever sees us with an evil eye,
When he plants may the floods sweep his mounds away.
Whoever wishes us evil,
May he break his fist on the ground.
We are broody hens, we have chicks.
We do not fly up,

We look after our brood.
We do not eye others with an evil eye.
This big-headed thing [child] that came home yesterday,
He is yet a seed.
If you wish that he germinates
And grows to be a tree,
We shall be ever thankful.
Earth Goddess, hear;
He will grow to be like his stock.

(Nigeria, date unknown)

Prayer for a New Son

Now that it's over, Lord, thank You,
because both my wife and my little boy
are doing just fine,
I've even seen him already,
in one of those incubators,
fed and wrinkled
and, to me, totally beautiful.

You wouldn't think something that small
could be alive,
but he is,
shaking his midget fists at the world
and screaming:
Look out, I'm here.

He is here, Lord, all here,
yet the world won't look out,
and he won't have that glass hothouse
to protect him like a rose.

He'll have to grow up,
and be stepped on,
and stand alone against the rain of knocks
the world is always too ready to provide.
So be with him, Lord, as I will,
at least long enough
to see his own image made over
in the joy of a first child.

(Max Pauli, Christian, modern)

For the Birth of a Daughter

God, we thank you that she is beautiful,
with her squinched up eyes and her tiny, tiny toes.
She is beautiful because she is ours,
or so we think now.
Yet from the beginning we must start giving her up
so that she can be herself.

We must love her but not smother her.
We must care for her and protect her
but not keep her too close.
We want her to live and love and be herself.
We know that she will experience hurt and heartache
that we cannot prevent.
She will also find beauty,
hear an inner music,
and walk on the wind.

Right now she seems completely and dependably ours.
We are glad to know such a feeling.

Touch her and us with the finger of your Spirit
So that in our life together
    we may enrich each other.

(Kenneth G. Phifer, modern)

Dedicating a Baby to God

To thee, the Creator, to thee, the Powerful,
I offer this fresh bud, new fruit of the ancient tree.
Thou art the master, we thy children.
To thee, the Creator, to thee, the Powerful,
Khmvoum [God], Khmvoum,
I offer this new plant.

(Pygmies, Zaire, date unknown)

Carrying Out of a Child

(Done in the fourth month outdoors while facing the rising sun.)

That eye-like luminary, the cause of blessings to the gods rises in the east; may we behold it for a hundred years. May we hear, may we speak, may we be free from poverty for a hundred years or more.

(Hindu, Rig-Veda *VII.66.16;* Vājasaneyi-Samhita *XXXVI.24)*

A Child Is Introduced to the Universe

*(A supplication to the powers of the heavens, air,
and earth for the safety of a child from birth to old age,
performed on a child's eighth day.)*

Ho! Ye Sun, Moon, Stars, all ye that move in the heavens.
  I bid you hear me!
Into your midst has come a new life.
  Consent ye, I implore!
Make its path smooth, that it may reach the brow of the first hill!

Ho! Ye Winds, Clouds, Rain, Mist, all ye that move in the air,
  I bid you hear me!
Into your midst has come a new life.
  Consent ye, I implore!
Make its path smooth, that it may reach the Brow of the second hill!

Ho! Ye Hills, Valleys, Rivers, Lakes, Trees, Grasses, all ye of the earth,
  I bid you hear me!

Into your midst has come a new life.
    Consent ye, I implore!
Make its path smooth, that it may reach the brow of the third hill!

Ho! Ye Birds, great and small, that fly in the air,
Ho! Ye Animals, great and small, that dwell in the forest,
Ho! Ye insects that creep among the grasses and burrow in the
    ground—
    I bid you hear me!
Into your midst has come a new life.
    Consent ye, I implore!
Make its path smooth, that it may reach the brow of the fourth hill!

Ho! All ye of the heavens, all ye of the air, all ye of the earth:
    I bid you all to hear me!
Into your midst has come a new life.
    Consent ye, consent ye all, I implore!
Make its path smooth—then shall it travel beyond the four hills!

(Omaha, date unknown)

Presenting an Infant to the Sun

*(Performed on the tenth day of age by the mother
and paternal grandmother.)*

Now this is the day.
Our child,
Into the daylight
You will go out standing.
Preparing for your day,
We have passed our days.
When all your days were at an end,
When eight days were past,
Our sun father
Went in to sit at his sacred place.
And our night fathers,
Having come standing to their sacred place,
Passing a blessed night.
Now this day,
Our fathers, Dawn priests,
Have come standing to their sacred place,
Our sun father,

Having come out standing to his sacred place,
Our child, it is your day.
This day,
The flesh of the white corn, prayer meal,
To our sun father
This prayer meal we offer.

May your road be fulfilled.
Reaching to the road of your sun father,
When your road is fulfilled,
In your thoughts may we live,
May we be the ones whom your thoughts will embrace,
For this, on this day
To our sun father,
We offer prayer meal.
To this end:
May you help us all to finish our roads.

(Zuñi, date unknown)

Presentation of a Child

Abousaye [gently]! *Akhwari* [sweetly]! Here is the child. Let him grow tall, let him grow into manhood with your medicines. Let his sweat be pure, let the stains go, let them go to Chibouri, let them go to Nkhabelane! Let the child play happily, let him be like his friends. This is not my first try. You gave me these medicines: let them protect the child against sickness so that no one can say they are powerless.

(South Africa, date unknown)

Blessing of a Baptismal Font

Make thyself manifest, O Lord, in this water and grant to him who is baptized in it so to be transformed, that he may put off the old man, which is corrupted by deceitful lusts, and may put on the new man, which is formed fresh according to the image of the Creator. Grafted through baptism into the likeness of thy death, may he become a partaker also in thy resurrection. May he guard the gift of thy Holy Spirit, may he increase the measure of grace which has been entrusted to him, and so may he receive the prize which is God's calling to life above, being numbered among the first born whose names are written in heaven.

(Christian, Eastern Orthodox, date unknown)

Baptism

Blessed is God, who desires that all men should be saved and come to the knowledge of the truth.

Blessed is God, who gives light and sanctification to every man that comes into the world.

Blessed are they whose transgressions are forgiven and whose sins are covered: blessed is the man to whom the Lord imputes no sin, and in whose mouth there is no deceit.

O Christ our God, rich in mercy, who clothest thyself with light as with a garment, grant unto me a robe that is radiant with light.

(Christian, Eastern Orthodox, date unknown)

Prayer for Baptism

God of eternal truth and love,
Vouchsafe the promised aid we claim;
Thine own great ordinance approve,
The child baptized into thy name
Partaker of thy nature make,
And give him all thine image back.

Father, if such thy sovereign will,
If Jesus did the rite enjoin,
Annex they hallowing Spirit's seal,
And let the grace attend the sign;
The seed of endless life impart,
Take for thine own this infant's heart.

In presence of thy heavenly host
Thyself we faithfully require:
Come, Father, Son, and Holy Ghost,
By blood, by water and by fire,
And fill up all thy human shrine,
And seal our souls for ever thine.

(Charles Wesley, Christian, 1707–1788)

Baptism of a Child

O God of infinite mercy, be pleased to grant unto this child an understanding mind and a sanctified heart. May thy providence lead him through the dangers, temptations, and ignorance of his youth, that he may never run into folly, nor into the evils of an unbridled appetite. We pray thee so to order the course of his life that, by good education, by holy examples, and by thy restraining and renewing grace, he may be led to serve thee faithfully all his days, through Jesus Christ our Lord.

(Christian, date unknown)

Baptism of a Child

Almighty and most merciful Father, who claimest the children as thy heritage, and who hast established an everlasting covenant with thy people and with their children: we beseech thee graciously to receive and bless this child, whom his parents now dedicate to thee. As, in thy name, he is baptized with the baptism of water, do thou endow him with the gift of the Holy Spirit. Accept him for thine own; set upon him the consecrating seal of thy covenant; and evermore endue him with thy heavenly grace; that to his life's end he may glorify thee with body and spirit; through Jesus Christ our Lord.

(Hubert Simpson, modern)

Baptism of Adults

Almighty and Everliving God, the aid of all that need, the helper of all that flee to thee for succor, the life of them that believe, and the resurrection of the dead: we call upon thee for these persons, that they, coming to the Holy Baptism, may also be filled with the Holy Spirit. Receive them, O Lord, as thou hast promised by thy well-beloved Son, saying, Ask, and ye shall receive; seek, and ye shall find; knock, and it shall be opened unto you. So give now unto us that ask; let us that seek, find; open the gate unto us that knock; that these persons may enjoy the everlasting benediction of thy heavenly washing, and may come to the eternal kingdom which thou has promised, by Jesus Christ our Lord.

(Christian, date unknown)

At the Ceremony of Washing an Infant

(Performed at four months of age.)

God! Give us health.
God! Protect us.
And you our spirits, protect us for this child.

(Nandi, Kenya, date unknown)

Confirmation

Almighty and everliving God, who has vouchsafed to regenerate these thy servants by water and the Holy Ghost, and hast given unto them forgiveness of all their sins: Strengthen them, we beseech thee, O Lord, with the Holy Ghost the comforter, and daily increase in them thy manifold gifts of grace; the spirit of wisdom and understanding; the spirit of counsel and ghostly strength; the spirit of knowledge and true godliness; and fill them, O Lord, with the spirit of thy holy fear, now and for ever.

(Christian, date unknown)

Parents' Prayer for a Bar or Bat Mitzvah

Into our hands, O God, You have placed Your Torah, to be held high by parents and children, and taught by one generation to the next.

Whatever has befallen us, our people have remained steadfast in loyalty to the Torah. It was carried into exile in the arms of parents that their children might not be deprived of their birthright.

And now I pray that you, my child, will always be worthy of this inheritance. Take its teaching into your heart, and in turn pass it on to your children and those who come after you. May you be a faithful Jew, searching for wisdom and truth, working for justice and peace. Thus will you be among those who labor to bring nearer the day when the Lord shall be One and His name shall be One.

(Jewish, date unknown)

Songs of Maturation for a Girl's Puberty Rites

(White Painted Woman symbolizes the feminine principle.)

1.
I come to White Painted Woman,
By means of long life I come to her.
I come to her by means of her blessing,
I come to her by means of her good fortune,
I come to her by means of all her different fruits.
By means of the long life she bestows, I come to her.
By means of this holy truth she goes about.

2.
I am about to sing this song of yours,
The song of long life.
Sun, I stand here on the earth with your song,
Moon, I have come in with your song.

3.
White Painted Woman's power emerges,
Her power for sleep.

White Painted Woman carries this girl;
She carries her through long life,
She carries her to good fortune,
She carries her to old age,
She bears her to peaceful sleep.

4.
You have started out on the good earth;
You have started out with good moccasins;
With moccasin strings of the rainbow, you have started out.
With moccasin strings of the sun rays, you have started out.
In the midst of plenty you have started out.

(Chiricahua, date unknown)

Talking God Hogan Song No. 25

(Blessing Way for a Girl's Puberty Rites)

With my sacred power, I am traveling.
With my sacred power, I am traveling.
With my sacred power, I am traveling.

At the back of my house, white shell prayer offerings are placed;
     they are beautifully decorated;
   With my sacred power, I am traveling,
At the center of my house, turquoise prayer offerings are placed;
     they are beautifully decorated;
   With my sacred power, I am traveling,
In my house by the fireside, abalone prayer offerings are placed;
     they are beautifully decorated;
   With my sacred power I am traveling,
In my house, in the corners by the door,
     black jewel prayer offerings are placed;
   With my sacred power, I am traveling,
In the doorway of my house, rock crystal prayer offerings are placed;
     they are beautifully decorated;
   With my sacred power, I am traveling.

All about my house is Talking God; He is beautifully clad;
  With my sacred power, I am traveling.
All about my house is Hogan God; She is beautifully clad;
  With my sacred power, I am traveling.
All about my house, bushes are growing;
    they are beautifully leafed out;
  With my sacred power I am traveling.
All about my house, trees are growing;
    they are beautifully leafed out;
  With my sacred power, I am traveling.
All about my house, rocks are standing;
    their surfaces are beautiful;
  With my sacred power I am traveling.
All about my house, mountains are standing;
    their sides are beautiful;
  With my sacred power, I am traveling.
All about my house, springs are flowing; they are beautiful;
  With my sacred power, I am traveling.
All about my house is White Corn Boy; He is beautifully clad;
  With my sacred power, I am traveling.
All about my house is Yellow Corn Girl; She is beautifully clad;
  With my sacred power, I am traveling.
All about my house is Corn Pollen Boy; He is beautifully clad;
  With my sacred power, I am traveling.
All about my house is Corn Beetle Girl; She is beautifully clad;
  With my sacred power, I am traveling.

With beauty before me, I am traveling,
    With my sacred power I am traveling,
With beauty behind me, I am traveling,
    With my sacred power, I am traveling,
With beauty below me, I am traveling,
    With my sacred power, I am traveling,
With beauty above me, I am traveling,
    With my sacred power, I am traveling,
Now with long life, now with everlasting beauty, I live.
    I am traveling,
    With my sacred power, I am traveling,

    With my sacred power, I am traveling,
    With my sacred power, I am traveling,
    With my sacred power, I am traveling, it is said.

(Navajo, date unknown)

7

Children

Thanksgiving for Our Children

Almighty God and heavenly Father, we thank thee for the children which thou hast given us; give us also the grace to train them in thy faith, fear, and love, that as they advance in years they may grow in grace, and may hereafter be found in the number of thine elect children; through Jesus Christ our Lord.

(Bishop Cosin, Christian, date unknown)

A Parent's Invocation to Build Immunity into the Life Scroll of the Little One

Father, Thou art love. Thou art the love of the Universe. Thou dost express thy love in perfect life, perfect health and strength and vigor. Life, in its perfection and fullness, is a manifestation of Thy perfect love. Thou are in the deathless, indestructible spirit of man. And any life filled with Thy love need not fear the deadly pestilence. Father, I thank Thee that there can be nothing between Thy life-perfecting-presence and this Thy little one.

(Herbert Coolidge, modern)

A Parent's Invocation for a Child's Guidance to Good Habits

My child, I love you. I pour out the full flow of my mother's [or father's] love upon your perfect and responsive spirit, that perfect and responsive spirit within you which is of God. I love you! I love you! I love you! There is unity between us and unison with God.

Father, thou art love. Thou art the all-God of the universe. Thou art the great power of perfection which manifests itself resistlessly in answer to selfless, loving prayer. I thank Thee that Thou art the loving-guidance-in-selection of my little one. I thank Thee that through Thy indwelling intelligence he will choose always the things that are good for the body, mind and soul.

(Herbert Coolidge, modern)

For Youth

Our Father, we give Thee thanks for our boys and girls with their fresh outlook upon life and their wealth of potential resources. Bless them with Thine own presence as they graduate from our schools and colleges at this season of the year. Grant that they may remember their Creator in the days of their youth. Make them mindful of the meaning which Thou alone canst give life. Help them to dedicate themselves to noble service and to high ideals. Grant them the satisfaction of genuine success and the joy of real accomplishment in the years ahead, we ask in Jesus' name.

(Stuart R. Oglesby, Christian, modern)

A Mother's Prayer

Starting forth on life's rough way,
　　Father, guide them;
O! We know not what of harm
　　May betide them;
'Neath the shadow of Thy wing,
　　Father, hide them;
Waking, sleeping, Lord, we pray,
　　God beside them.

When in prayer they cry to Thee,
　　Do Thou hear them;
From the stains of sin and shame
　　Do Thou clear them:
'Mid the quicksands and the rocks,
　　Do Thou steer them;
In Temptation, trial, grief,
　　Be Thou near them.

Unto Thee we give them up,
　　Lord, receive them;

In the word we know must be
Much to grieve them—
Many striving oft and strong
To deceive them;
Trustful in Thy hands of love
We must leave them.

(William Cullen Bryant, 1794–1878)

A Cradle Song

Sweet dreams, form a shade
O'er my lovely infant's head;
Sweet dreams of pleasant streams
By happy, silent, moony beams.

Sweet sleep, with soft down
Weave thy brows an infant crown.
Sweet sleep, Angel mild,
Hover o'er my happy child.

Sweet smiles, in the night
Hover over my delight;
Sweet smiles, Mother's smiles,
All the livelong night beguiles.

Sweet moans, dove like sighs,
Chase not slumber from thy eyes.
Sweet moans, sweeter smiles,
All the dove like moans beguiles.

Sleep, sleep, happy child,
All creation slept and smil'd;
Sleep, sleep, happy sleep,
While o'er thee thy mother weep.

Sweet babe, in thy face.
Holy image I can trace.
Sweet babe, once like thee,
Thy maker lay and wept for me,

Wept for me, for thee, for all,
When he was an infant small.
Thou his image ever see,
Heavenly face that smiles on thee,

Smiles on thee, on me, on all;
Who became an infant small.
Infant smiles are his own smiles;
Heaven & earth to peace beguiles.

(William Blake, 1757–1827)

Bless My Children

Bless our children with healthful bodies, with good understandings, with the graces and gifts of thy Spirit, with sweet dispositions and holy habits; and sanctify them throughout in their bodies, souls, and spirits, and keep them unblameable to the coming of our Lord Jesus.

(Jeremy Taylor, Christian, 1613–1667)

When Putting a Child to Sleep

Waking, may my babe rise safe:
Sleeping, may God give him health.

(Christian, date unknown)

A Parent's Prayer

O Almighty God, and heavenly Father, of whom the whole family in heaven, and on earth is named, make me, I beseech Thee, a kind a tender parent, and truly careful and solicitous to promote the welfare and happiness of my children. Let thy Holy Spirit assist me to form in their tender minds the principles of virtue and religion, to teach them to remember Thee their creator, in the days of their youth, to instruct them in thy fear and love, and to bring them up in the nurture and admonition of the Lord. Let me make it my constant care and endeavor to wean them from all pride and vanity, and to set before their eyes the example of a holy and religious life.

(Rev. James Ford, b. 1824)

A Teen's Prayer to Become like God

Father, O mighty force,
That force which is in everything,
Come down between us, fill us,
Until we be like thee,
Until we be like thee.

(Guinea, date unknown)

8

Friends and Loved Ones

For Friends

O Fountain of Love, love thou our friends and teach them to love thee with all their hearts, that they may think and speak and do only such things as are well pleasing to thee; through Jesus Christ our Lord.

(St. Anselm, Christian, 1033–1109)

For Friends

Almighty God, by Whose goodness we were created, and Whose mercies never fail; we commend to Thee all who have a place in our hearts and sympathies; all who are joined to us by the sacred ties of kindred, friendship and love; all little children who are dear to us; all who help us to a faithful life and whose spirit turn our duties into love; keep them both outwardly in their bodies and inwardly in their souls, and pour upon them the continual dew of Thy blessing.

(Rev. J. Hunter, b. 1849)

For Neighbors and Friends

O God of Love, we pray thee give us love: love in our thinking, love in our speaking, love in our doing, and love in the hidden places of our souls; love of our neighbors, near and far; love of our friends, old and new; love of those with whom we find it hard to bear, and love of those who find it hard to bear with us; love of those with whom we work, and love of those with whom we take our ease; love in joy, and love in sorrow; love in life, and love in death: that so at length we may be worthy to dwell with thee, who art Eternal Love.

(Christian, date unknown)

For Those We Love

Almighty God, by whose goodness we were created, and whose mercies never fail, we commend to thee all who have a place in our hearts and sympathies; all who are joined to us by the sacred ties of kindred, friendship, and love; keep them both outwardly in their bodies and inwardly in their souls.

(John Hunter, 1849–1917)

Charity Toward Neighbors

Grant, O my Savior, that I may observe, with the greatest care, Thy precept of charity towards my neighbor, to love him as Thou hast loved us, since this is absolutely necessary for salvation. Give me also that tenderness of charity which may prevent me from wounding it in any way: for Thou hast said that to offend our neighbor is to wound the apple of Thine eye. Grant, therefore, that I may avoid Thy displeasure by not incurring the displeasure of my neighbor.

(Thomas à Kempis, Christian, 1380–1471)

To Find Our Hearts Ready

Lord our God, may love and kindness, peace and happiness dwell among us. May we live always among good friends, and be to them faithful companions. May we have hope of goodness in the future, and awaken each morning to find our hearts ready to serve You.

(Jewish, date unknown)

Especially for Friends

O blessed Lord, who hast commanded us to love one another, grant us grace that having received thine undeserved bounty, we may love everyone in thee and for thee. We implore thy clemency for all; but especially for the friends whom thy love has given to us. Love thou them, O thou fountain of love, and make them to love thee with all their heart, that they may will, and speak, and do those things only which are pleasing to thee.

(St. Anselm, Christian, 1033–1109)

For Friends

B e pleased, O Lord, to remember my friends, all that have prayed for me, and all that have done me good. Do thou good to them, and return all their kindness double into their own bosom, rewarding them with blessings, and sanctifying them with thy graces, and bringing them to glory.

(Jeremy Taylor, Christian, 1613–1667)

For Friends and Kindred

O Thou, who art the God of all the families of the earth; We beseech thee to bless all our friends and kindred, wherever they may be, especially (names), and grant that we may ever be knit together in bonds of mutual love.

(Christian, date unknown)

A Blessing for Loved Ones

O God, Who by the grace of the Holy Ghost hast poured the gifts of love into our hearts; Grant unto my friends and kindred, especially (names) health of body and soul, and every spiritual gift; that they may love Thee with all their strength, and with perfect affection fulfill Thy pleasure.

(Christian, date unknown)

Love for Others

How big and beautiful
Are the hearts of those
Who put first
The welfare of others—
Yes, even before their own.

I am doing my best
In my desire to fulfill
The needs and wants
Of all humanity,
And to make others happy.

Know that the happiness
Which we feel when we bring joy
And make others happy,
Is a greater happiness
Than any on earth.

(Japanese, date unknown)

9

School

Going to School

O Lord, who is the fountain of all wisdom and learning, you have given me the years of my youth to learn the arts and skills necessary for an honest and holy life. Enlighten my mind, that I may acquire knowledge. Strengthen my memory, that I may retain what I have learnt. Govern my heart, that I may always be eager and diligent in my studies. And let your Spirit of truth, judgement and prudence guide my understanding, that I may perceive how everything I learn fits into your holy plan for the world.

(John Calvin, Christian, 1509–1564)

For Students and Teachers

Grant, O Lord, to all teachers and students, to know that which is worth knowing, to love that which is worth loving, to praise that which pleaseth thee most, and to dislike whatsoever is evil in thine eyes. Grant us with true judgment to distinguish things that differ, and above all to search out and to do what is well-pleasing unto thee; through Jesus Christ our Lord.

(Thomas à Kempis, Christian, 1380–1471)

Graduation Day

O Master, we thank Thee for the fresh young lives of our boys and girls, trained in our schools, and now ready to set forth into the world to find their places of service. Guide them, unerringly, with Thy hand into the work which Thou hast appointed them. Let none hold life lightly, nor carelessly spend the precious years allotted them. May all, grateful for their opportunities, mindful of their responsibilities, and eager for heroic and unselfish tasks in a distracted world, be used by the Lord of men and nations in carrying to completion His wise and loving plans. For Jesus' sake.

(Stuart R. Oglesby, Christian, modern)

Blessing for Places of Learning

O God, who art the only Source of light and wisdom, be pleased to shed forth thy spirit upon all universities, colleges, schools, and places of learning, with their professors, teachers, and students, and so to prosper their studies that they may finally come into the perfect knowledge of thee, whom to know is life everlasting.

(John Watson, Christian, date unknown)

For a School

Holy spirit, help us in this school, to live together in love and peace, patient with each other's faults and mindful of each other's wants. May we be gentle in words and helpful in deeds, not seeking our own profit only, but rather the good of all. Fill our hearts and minds so completely with thy presence that they may compel us to love one another.

(Christian, date unknown)

For a School

Almighty God, in whom we live and move and have our being, make this school as a field which the Lord hath blessed, that whatsoever things are true, pure, lovely, and of good report may here for ever flourish and abound. Preserve in it an unblemished name, enlarge it with a wider usefulness, and exalt it in the love and reverence of all its members as an instrument of thy glory, for the sake of Jesus Christ, our Lord.

(Henry Hayman, 1823–1904)

For Schools and Schoolchildren

Grant, we beseech thee, O Lord Jesus, that all those in our schools may seek to find out what thou wouldest have them to do in life, and earnestly strive to follow thee, who in thy boyhood didst choose to do thy Father's business; for thy name's sake.

(Christian, date unknown)

For School

O God, from whom every good and perfect gift doth come, give us grace to consecrate to thy service the talents which thou hast committed to our charge, that, whether as teachers or learners, we may do all things as in thy sight and to thy glory.

(Christian, date unknown)

10

Work

My Work

Master, give me the courage to follow thy lead when I hear Thy voice calling and directing my work. May I never fail to come and to do my work with singleness of heart for thy dear sake. May the little difficulties I now think so serious melt and disappear in the happiness that comes from being one spirit with Thee and with those who stand ready to be used for Thy plans. Keep me from temptation and impatience and every evil thing, and help me always to seek Thy face.

(Elinor Cochrane Stewart, modern)

Before Work

My God, you are always close to me. In obedience to you, I must now apply myself to outward things. Yet, as I do so, I pray that you will give me the grace of your presence. And to this end I ask that you will assist my work, receive its fruits as an offering to you, and all the while direct all my affections to you.

(Brother Lawrence, Christian, 1611–1691)

Going to Work

My God, Father and Preserver, who in your goodness has watched over me in this past night and brought me to this day, grant that I may spend the day wholly in your service. Let me not think or say or do a single thing that is not obedience to your will; but rather let all my actions be directed to your glory and the salvation of my brethren. Let me attempt nothing that is not pleasing to you; but rather let me seek happiness only in your grace and goodness. Grant also, that as I labour for the goods and clothing necessary for this life, I may constantly raise my mind upwards to the heavenly life which you promise to all your children.

(John Calvin, Christian, 1509–1564)

For One's Work to Prosper

Almighty God, have mercy on me.
May this child of mine see these things,
So that my work may be seen by all men,
And also those who do not trust me,
May their infidelity change!

(Meru, Kenya, date unknown)

On Going to Work

Give me, dear Lord, a pure heart and a wise mind, that I may carry out my work according to your will. Save me from all false desires, from pride, greed, envy and anger, and let me accept joyfully every task you set before me. Let me seek to serve the poor, the sad and those unable to work. Help me to discern honestly my own gifts that I may do the things of which I am capable, and happily and humbly leave the rest to others. Above all, remind me constantly that I have nothing except what you give me, and can do nothing except what you enable me to do.

(Jacob Boehme, Christian, 1575–1624)

Work

P rosper thou the works of my hands, O Lord; O, prosper thou my handiwork.

(Thomas Ken, Christian, 1637–1711)

For Results

Lord, give me the grace to work to bring about the things that I pray for.

(St. Thomas More, Christian, 1478–1535)

That Our Work May Be a Delight

O Lord, renew our spirits and draw our hearts unto thyself that our work may not be to us a burden, but a delight; and give us such mighty love to thee as may sweeten all our obedience. O, let us not serve thee with the spirit of bondage as slaves, but with the cheerfulness and gladness of children, delighting ourselves in thee and rejoicing in thy work.

(Benjamin Jenks, Christian, 1646–1724)

Let Us Rejoice

Let us rejoice in the light of day, in the glory and warmth of the sun, in the reawakening of life to duty and labor.

We rejoice in the light of day.

In the quiet night, with its rest from toil and its revelation of worlds beyond the dark.

We rejoice in the peace of night.

In the earth with its hills and valleys, its widespread fields of grain, its fruit and hidden treasures.

We rejoice in the beauty of earth.

We rejoice in the strength to win our daily bread, and in homes where we find refuge from the cold and storm.

We rejoice in the shelter of home.

In the love of fathers and mothers who have nurtured our lives, with whose blessing we have gone forth to our own work in the world.

We rejoice in the love of our parents.

In the children who bless our homes, whose eager minds and
hearts are the promise of tomorrow.

We rejoice in our children.

In friends who share our sorrows and joys, in the fullness of the
abundant life, in the serenity of old age, and in the peace that
comes at last.

We rejoice, and will rejoice for evermore.

(Jewish, modern)

In the Marketplace

Lord, give me grace to use this world so as not to abuse it. Lord, grant that I may never go beyond or defraud my brother in any matter, for thou art the avenger of all such.

(Thomas Ken, Christian, 1637–1711)

11

Pets and Animals

To Be Kind

O Lord Jesus Christ, Who hast taught us that without our Father in heaven no sparrow falls to the ground, help us to be very kind to all animals and to our pets. May we remember that Thou wilt one day ask us if we have been good to them. Bless us as we take care of them. For Thy sake.

(Christian, date unknown)

For Our Friends the Animals

Hear our humble prayer, O God, for our friends the animals. We entreat for them all thy mercy and pity, and for those who deal with them we ask a heart of compassion and gentle hands and kindly words. Make us ourselves to be true friends to animals and so to share the blessing of the merciful. For the sake of thy Son, the tender-hearted, Jesus Christ our Lord.

(Russian prayer, date unknown)

Prayer for Puppies

Maker of the animals,
we pray today for little pups.
We praise you
that even their blindness and whining
are ways of happiness in this world.

May they never be alone and cold.
May their wishes for a friendly home
be speedily fulfilled.
And spare them please all curiosity
for fast-moving machines.

Help us to see in these spots on our rug
little tokens of that baptism
into a new and special life
shared only with a dog.

And teach us forgiveness
through countless ruined shoes
and other chewings.

In this fluffy gift,
grant us glimpses of that inheritance
reserved especially for the meek,
gladden our hearts
with the licks and wiggles
of spontaneous love,
and teach us the meaning of sniffs,
scratches, and wagging tails.

We lift this bit of life before you
and ask you to deliver us now
from ringworm, fleas,
and cats that won't scare.

(Robert Jones, modern)

Tenderness Towards All

O God, source of life and power, Who feedeth the birds of the heavens, increase our tenderness towards all the creatures of Thy hand. Help us to refrain from petty acts of cruelty, or thoughtless deeds of harm to any living animal. May we care for them at all times, especially during hard weather, and protect them from injury so that they learn to trust us as friends. Let our sympathy grow with knowledge, so that the whole creation may rejoice in Thy presence.

(Christian, date unknown)

For Animals

O merciful Father, who has given life to many and lovest all that thou has made, give us the spirit of thine own loving kindness that we may show mercy to all helpless creatures. Especially would we pray for those which minister to our sport or comfort, that they may be treated with tenderness of hands, in thankfulness of heart, and that we may discover thee, the Creator, in all created things.

(Christian, date unknown)

The Unfledged Bird

Have pity, O Lord God, lest they who go by the way trample on the unfledged bird, and send thine Angel to replace it in the nest, that it may live till it can fly.

(St. Augustine, Christian, 354–430)

For Animals

For those, O Lord, the humble beasts, that bear with us the burden and heat of the day, and offer their guileless lives for the well-being of their countries; and for the wild creatures, whom thou hast made wise, strong and beautiful; we supplicate for them thy great tenderness of heart, for thou hast promised to save both man and beast, and great is thy loving kindness, O Master, Saviour of the world.

(Christian, Eastern Church, date unknown)

For the Suffering of Animals

Hear our humble prayer, O God, for our friends the animals, thy creatures. We pray especially for all that are suffering in any way; for the overworked and underfed, the hunted, lost or hungry; for all in captivity or ill-treated, and for those who must be put to death.

We entreat for them Thy mercy and pity; and for those who deal with them we ask a heart of compassion, gentle hands and kindly words.

Make us all to be true friends to animals.

(Christian, date unknown)

12

Travel and Safety

For Protection

God, who are the only hope of the world, the only refuge for unhappy men, abiding in the perfect harmony of heaven, give me courage and strength in the midst of the conflicts here on earth. Protect me from the utter ruin that would befall me if my weak faith gave way under the many blows which assail me. Remember that I am mere dust and wind and shadow, whose life is as fleeting as that of a wild flower in the grass. But may your eternal mercy, which has shone since time began, rescue me from the jaws of evil.

(Bede, Christian, c. 672–735)

Before a Journey

Go before thy servant this day;
   if Thou thyself go not forth with me,
      carry me not up hence.
Thou, who didst guide the Israelites by an Angel,
      the wise men by a star;
   who didst preserve Peter in the waves,
      and Paul in the shipwreck;
be present with me, O Lord, and dispose my way;
go with me, and lead me out, and lead me back.

(Bishop Lancelot Andrewes, Christian, 1555–1626)

For a Journey

Hear our prayers, Lord, and give your servants a safe and happy journey; and may your help be with them in all the changes and chances of their way through this life.

(Christian, date unknown)

For a Safe Journey

Gently! Smoothly! I say so. Death does not come to him for whom prayer is made; death only comes to him who trusts in his own strength! Let misfortune depart, let it go to Shiburi, and Nkhabelane. Let him travel safely; let him trample on his enemies; let thorns sleep, let lions sleep; let him drink water wherever he goes, and let that water make him happy, by the strength of his herb.

(Central or southern Africa, date unknown)

For Travellers

O Thou who art the confidence of the ends of the earth, and of them that are afar off upon the sea, we commend to thine Almighty protection all travellers by sea and land, overshadow them by thy mercy, and surround them with thy love. When they cry unto thee in distress, do thou mercifully send them help and deliverance. Go with them on their journey, and grant to those who are afar from their homes that they may revisit them, in thy good name, in peace.

(Christian, date unknown)

Before a Temporary Separation

Today we go forth separate, some of us to pleasure, some of us to worship, some upon duty. Go with us, our guide and angel; hold thou before us in our divided paths the mark of our low calling, still to be true to what small best we can attain to. Help us in that, our maker, the dispenser of events—thou, of the vast designs, in which we blindly labor, suffer us to be so far constant to ourselves and our beloved.

(Robert Louis Stevenson, 1850–1894)

For General Protection

The light of God surrounds me;
The love of God enfolds me;
The power of God protects me;
The presence of God watches over me.
Wherever I am, God is!

(James Dillet Freeman, modern)

Breton Fisherman's Prayer

Dear God, be good to me,
The sea is so wide,
And my boat is so small.

(Christian, date unknown)

Going or Coming

Lord, bless my going out and coming in, from this time forth, for evermore.

(Thomas Ken, Christian, 1637–1711)

A Mother's Blessing

Be the great God between thy two shoulders
To protect thee in thy going and in thy coming.
Be the Son of Mary Virgin near thy heart,
And be the perfect Spirit upon thee pouring
Oh, the perfect Spirit upon thee pouring!

(Gaelic oral tradition, date unknown)

During a Journey

We give thanks to Thee, O God, our Creator and Preserver, for all Thy mercies continued to us through another day; for protection on our way, for deliverance from all perils and dangers, for bringing us in safety thus far on our journey [or to the end of our journey]; for all fair and glorious works of God or man we have seen, for all true and pure and good thoughts which have been put into our minds, for all opportunities of hearing, learning, or doing good, for continued health, for all the blessings of this life, and for all Thy gifts of grace.

(Christian, date unknown)

On a Trip

You, O God, are the Lord of the mountains and the valleys. As I travel over mountains and through valleys, I am beneath your feet. You surround me with every kind of creature. Peacocks, pheasants, and wild boars cross my path. Open my eyes to see their beauty, that I may perceive them as the work of your hands. In your power, in your thought, all things are abundant. Tonight I will sleep beneath your feet, O Lord of the mountains and valleys, ruler of the trees and vines. I will rest in your love, with your protecting me as a father protects his children, with you watching over me as a mother watches over her children. Then tomorrow the sun will rise and I will not know where I am; but I know that you will guide my footsteps.

(Sioux, date unknown)

For Friends and Loved Ones Preparing to Travel

O God of infinite mercy and unbounded majesty, whom no distance of place or lapse of time doth separate from those whom thou dost defend; be present with Thy servant who trusteth in Thee, and vouchsafe to be his Guide and Companion through the way by which he is about to go; that no adversity may do him hurt, no difficulty hinder him; but that all things may be favourable and prosperous unto him; that whatsoever he rightly and lawfully desires, he may speedily and effectually obtain.

(Christian, date unknown)

For Absent Friends

O God, who art everywhere present, look down with thy mercy upon those who are absent from among us. Give thy holy angels charge over them, and grant that they may be kept safe in body, soul and spirit, and presented faultless before the presence of thy glory with exceeding joy; through Jesus Christ our Lord.

(Bishop Brooke Foss Westcott, Christian, 1825–1901)

For Absent Loved Ones

O Lord our God, who art in every place, from whom no space or distance can ever separate us, we know that those who are absent from each other are present with thee, and we therefore pray thee to have in thy holy keeping those dear ones from whom we are now separated, and grant that both they and we, by drawing nearer unto thee, may be drawn nearer to each other, bound together by the unseen chain of thy love, in the communion of thy spirit, and in the holy friendship of thy saints.

(Sir William Martin, date unknown)

For Well-Being

May the road rise to meet you.
May the wind be always at your back.
May the sun shine warm upon your face.
May the rains fall softly upon your fields until we meet again.
May God hold you in the hollow of his hand.

(Gaelic oral tradition, date unknown)

Prayer for Safe Travel

God of distance and motion,
be with us now as we travel
this unfamiliar road.
Keep us alert as the sky darkens
and we are enveloped
by the massive shadows of the hills.

Give us the starlight, streetlight, porchlight
for our guides.
Give us inner light.
Give us your own light.
Give us a road that takes us
where we want to go.

Lift our hearts beyond the loneliness
of these strange vistas.
Keep us curious and interested
in what we may find around the next bend.
And calm any anxiety

over how we will be received
when at last we arrive.

Include us now among your people
who were happy to call themselves travelers,
and grant us the sense that you move with us
everywhere we go.

(Robert Jones, modern)

Faith

Lead kindly light, amid the encircling gloom,
   Lead Thou me on!
The night is dark, and I am far from home—
   Lead Thou me on!
Keep thou my feet; I do not ask to see
The distant scene—one step enough for me.

I was not ever thus, nor prayed that Thou
   Should'st lead me on.
I loved to choose and see my path; but now
   Lead Thou me on!
I loved the garish day, and, spite of fears,
Pride ruled my will: remember not past years!

So long Thy power hath blest me, sure it still
   Will lead me on,
O'er moor and fen, o'er crag and torrent, till
   The night is gone;
And with the morn those angel faces smile
Which I have loved long since, and lost awhile.

(Cardinal Newman, Christian, 1801–1890)

Acknowledgments and Permissions

Grateful acknowledgment is made to the authors and publishers for use of the following material. Every effort has been made to contact original sources.

"For a Wedding Anniversary" from *More Prayers for Plain People* by William Barclay. Copyright 1962 by William Barclay. Reprinted by permission of the publisher, Abingdon Press.

"Evening Blessing," "Let Us Rejoice," "To Find Our Hearts Ready" and "For a Bar or Bas Mitzvah" from *Gates of Prayer,* copyright 1975 by the Central Conference of American Rabbis. Used with permission.

"A Wedding Prayer" from *Divine Light of Salvation,* copyright 1984 by Mochiki Okada, by permission of the Johrei Fellowship.

"Prayer on Relatives" and "Prayer for a New Son" reprinted with permission from *Prayers for the Time Being* by Max Pauli, copyright 1974 by Ligouri Publications, Ligouri, MO 63057-999.

"Songs of Maturation" from *An Apache Life-Way,* copyright 1941 by Morris Edward Opler, the University of Chicago Press. Used by permission of Mrs. Lucille Opler for the estate of Morris Edward Opler.

Charlotte Johnson's Frisbie's "Talking God Hogan Song No. 25" from *Kinaalda,* copyright 1967 by Charlotte Johnson Frisbie and Wesleyan University Press, used by permission of University Press of New England.

"Prayer to Be Recited in the Morning" and "Recitation Before Meals" from *The Druze Faith,* copyright 1974 by Sami Nasib Marakem, used by permission of Caravan Books.

Bibliography

Appleton, George, ed. *The Oxford Book of Prayer.* Oxford: Oxford University Press, 1985.

Astrov, Margot, ed. *The Winged Serpent.* Boston: Beacon Press, 1992. First published 1946.

Bader, W., comp. *The Prayers of St. Francis.* Hyde Park, N.Y.: New City Press, 1994.

Barclay, William. *More Prayers for Plain People.* London: Wm. Collins Sons & Co., 1962.

A Book of Offices and Prayers for Priest and People. New York: Edwin S. Gorham, 1899.

Carr, Edwin Hamlin. *"Let Us Give Thanks."* New York: Fleming H. Revell Co. (a division of Baker Book House Company), 1929.

The Catholic Prayer Book. Ann Arbor, Mich.: Servant Publications, 1986.

Coolidge, Herbert. *Mother's Might and How to Use it.* Holyoke, Mass.: The Elizabeth Towne Co., 1919.

Cronyn, George W. *American Indian Poetry.* New York: Fawcett Columbine, 1962, 1991.

Davie, Donald. *The New Oxford Book of Christian Verse.* Oxford: Oxford University Press, 1988.

Fisher, A.S.T., comp. *An Anthology of Prayers.* London: Longmans, Green & Co., 1934.

Ford, Rev. James. *A Century of Christian Prayers on Faith, Hope and Charity; with a Morning and Evening Devotion.* 2nd ed. Ipswich, England: John Raw, 1824.

Fox, Selina Fitzherbert, comp. *A Chain of Prayer Across the Ages: Forty Centuries of Prayer, 2000 B.C.–A.D. 1941.* London: John Murray, 1913, 1941.

Frisbie, Charlotte Johnson. *Kinaalda: A Study of the Navaho Girl's Puberty Ceremony.* Middletown, Conn.: Wesleyan University Press, 1967.

Frost, S.E., Jr. *The Sacred Writings of the World's Great Religions.* New York: McGraw-Hill, 1943.

Frye, Northrop, ed. *Selected Poetry and Prose of William Blake.* New York: The Modern Library, 1953.

Gates of Prayer. New York: Central Conference of American Rabbis, 1975.

Goudge, Elizabeth. *A Diary of Prayer.* New York: Coward-McCann, 1966.

Hart, Rev. Samuel, comp. *A Manual of Short Daily Prayers for Families.* New York: Longmans, Green & Co., 1902.

Hernaman, Claudia Frances, comp. *The Itinerary: A Manual of Devotions for Travellers by Land and Sea.* London: Society for Promoting Christian Knowledge, 1889.

Jones, Robert. *Prayers for Puppies, Aging Autos, and Sleepless Nights.* Louisville, Ky.: Westminster/John Knox Press, 1990.

MacCrocaigh, R., trans. *Prayers of the Gael.* London: Sands & Co., 1914.

Makarem, Sami Nasib. *The Druze Faith.* Delmar, N.Y.: Caravan Books, 1974.

Martin, Hugh, ed. *A Book of Prayers for Schools.* London: Student Christian Movement Press, 1936.

Mbiti, John S. *The Prayers of African Religion.* Maryknoll, N.Y.: Orbis Books, 1975.

Morrow, Abbie C. *Prayers for Public Worship, Private Devotion, Personal Ministry.* New York: M.E. Munson, 1902.

The New Guideposts Treasury of Prayer. Carmel, N.Y.: Guideposts, 1991.

Newman, Richard, ed. *Bless All Thy Creatures, Lord.* New York: Macmillan Publishing Co., 1982.

Noyes, Morgan Phelps. *Prayers for Services.* New York: Charles Scribner's Sons, 1934.

Oglesby, Stuart R. *Prayers for All Occasions.* Louisville, Ky.: John Knox Press, 1940, 1989.

Okada, Mochiki. *Johrei: Divine Light of Salvation.* Kyoto, Japan: The Society of Johrei, 1984.

Page, Herman, and Gilbert Laidlaw, adapters and compilers. *Prayers.* New York: Edwin S. Gorham, 1918.

Pauli, Max. *Prayers for the Time Being.* Ligouri, Mo.: Ligouri Publications, 1974.

Phifer, Kenneth G. *A Book of Uncommon Prayer.* Nashville: The Upper Room, 1981.

Prayers Ancient and Modern. New York: Doubleday & McClure Co., 1897.

Ryan, Marah Ellis, comp. *Pagan Prayers.* Chicago: A.C. McClurg & Co., 1913.

Shorter, Aylward. *Prayer in the Religious Traditions of Africa.* London: Oxford University Press, 1975.

Sivananda, Swami. *Gems of Prayers.* Ananda Kutir, Rikhikesh: The Sivananda Publication League, 1943.

Stewart, Elinor Cochrane. *Prayers of Hope and Gladness.* New York: Pevensey Press, 1930.

Table Prayers for Daily Bread. South Bend, Ind.: Table Prayer League, 1917.

Thirkield, Wilbur Patterson, ed. and comp. *Service and Prayer for Church and Home.* New York: The Methodist Book Concern, 1918.

Thomas à Kempis. *The Imitation of Christ.* Rockford, Ill.: TAN Books and Publishers, 1989.

Tufte, Virginia, ed. *High Wedlock Then Be Honoured.* New York: The Viking Press, 1970.

Van de Weyer, Robert, comp. *The HarperCollins Book of Prayers.* San Francisco: HarperSanFrancisco, 1993.

The Voices of the Saints. Selected and arranged by Francis W. Johnston. Rockford, Ill.: TAN Books and Publishers, 1965.

Williams, Monier. *Religious Thought and Life in India.* New Delhi: Oriental Books Reprint Corp., 1974. First published 1883.

Wood, L.S. *A Book of English Verse on Infancy and Childhood.* London: Macmillan and Co. Ltd., 1921.

Woolley, Reginald Maxwell, trans. *Coptic Offices.* New York: The Macmillan Co., 1930.

Wordsworth, John. *Bishop Sarapion's Prayer-Book.* Hamden, Conn.: Archon Books, 1964.

PHOTO: LIGHTNER PHOTOGRAPHY, INC.

ROSEMARY ELLEN GUILEY is a renowned expert on spirituality, mystical and exceptional human experience, and the paranormal. She is a frequent and popular lecturer on such topics as angels, prayer, healing, dreams, alchemy, spiritual awakenings, and mysteries of the unknown. She serves on the board of trustees for the Academy of Religion and Psychical Research. Among her previous books are *The Miracle of Prayer, Angels of Mercy*, and *Tales of Reincarnation*, all published by Pocket Books. She lives with her husband near Annapolis, Maryland.